The Little Book of
Takoyaki

Little, Brown Lab
Hachette Book Group
1290 Avenue of the Americas, New York, NY 10104
littlebrownlab.com

First Edition: February 2019

Little, Brown Lab is an imprint of Little, Brown and
Company, a division of Hachette Book Group, Inc.
The Little, Brown Lab name and logo are trademarks
of Hachette Book Group, Inc.

Illustrations by Aimee Pong/OrangeYouGlad

ISBN 978-0-316-49412-0

The Little Book of
Takoyaki

Jessica Harlan

Illustrations by Aimee Pong

LITTLE,
BROWN
LAB

CONTENTS

INTRODUCTION

IN THE WORLD OF JAPANESE FOOD, some of the greatest pleasures are its many offerings of little snacks and nibbles. The Japanese counterpart to Spain's tapas, these snacks can range from dumplings to crispy bits of tempura to grilled meats on skewers. Takoyaki— traditional fried octopus balls—are not as common on menus as, say, dumplings or edamame, but they're a beloved and popular treat in certain parts of Japan. They're also starting to gain popularity in the United States.

What Is Takoyaki?

Takoyaki is straightforward when translated: *tako* means "octopus" and *yaki* means "grilled" or "fried."

Takoyaki originated in the city of Osaka in the mid-1930s, where, according to local lore, a street vendor was experimenting with a dough fritter that was popular at the time. He used octopus because it was plentiful in the city, and the use of wheat flour was still a novelty in a country where rice was king.

From there, Takoyaki evolved into what we know it as today: an octopus-studded ball of flavorful dough, cooked in a special pan of rounded cups. Takoyaki is typically crisp on the outside, and a little creamy on the inside, with chewy chunks of octopus. It's often served drizzled with a thick sweet-savory sauce and Japanese mayonnaise, and sprinkled with bonito flakes.

In Osaka, the history and tradition of takoyaki is so important to the city's culture that it's celebrated at a "museum" called Takopa Takoyaki Park. There, visitors can taste takoyaki from a number of different takoyaki shops, play carnival games, and learn about the history of takoyaki and how it's made.

All across Japan, you'll find takoyaki highlighted on restaurant menus, served at food stalls, and hawked by festival vendors. Some chefs prepare and serve it the traditional way, while others take liberties with the condiments, toppings, fillings, and seasonings.

Why Takoyaki?

It's fun: Mastering the technique of filling and flipping the balls in the takoyaki pan is lots of fun and lends itself to a lot of creativity. Mix up your favorite cake, muffin, pancake, or quick bread recipe and try cooking it in your takoyaki pan!

It's interactive: In Japan, takoyaki parties are a fun way of entertaining. The host sets out all the ingredients, and everyone gathers around the pan, pouring in the batter, adding the ingredients, and flipping the balls when they're ready. With the recipes in this book, you and your guests can have fun cooking and eating together.

It's fast: The smaller portion size and the concentrated heat mean the food cooks quickly. Most of the recipes in this book cook in a matter of minutes, and you can make 16 to 18 balls at a time, depending on how many cups your takoyaki pan has.

It's tasty: Traditional takoyaki is a delicious treat, full of contrasting flavors and textures. The variations on takoyaki in this book, as well as all the other recipes designed for your takoyaki pan, will delight adventurous eaters and tempt picky eaters alike.

Takoyaki at Home

That's why having your own takoyaki pan is so great! If you are a fan of the flavor and texture of takoyaki, you can re-create it at home and even get inventive with your pan to make a wide range of dishes. It's a super-fun and collaborative way of cooking for a group of friends or your family. All you need to do is set up an electric pan or a stovetop pan on a butane burner at the table, and get cooking! The technique is easy to master, and since takoyaki and other recipes made in the pan are best eaten hot and fresh, everyone will love eating them as they come off the pan!

On the American market, there are a few different options when it comes to takoyaki pans.

Stovetop Pans: These are the most common takoyaki pans. They're a good choice because they can fit on a typical gas burner and the temperature is easily controlled by simply turning your burner up or down. They're also easy to clean—some are even dishwasher safe! The Japanese often use this kind of pan with a portable butane burner (similar to a camp stove) so that they can cook at the table, which is a social and interactive way of eating takoyaki.

Stovetop takoyaki pans come in cast iron or aluminum. Cast iron takoyaki pans are heavier than aluminum ones and will take longer to get hot, but they retain heat better. Aluminum takoyaki pans are less expensive, lighter in weight, and respond more quickly to changes in temperature. Some Japanese manufacturers specify that their takoyaki pans are only for use on a tabletop burner from that supplier, but I've used my pan on my conventional gas stove with no issues. Some stovetop pans will also work on electric coils or induction cooktops, but if you plan to use one of these heat sources, be sure to check with the manufacturer first to make sure your pan is compatible.

Electric Pans: These are similar to countertop griddles that plug into an electrical socket and don't require an outside heat source. They have their own heating element below the metal plate with the round cups where you pour the batter. One issue with these is that most models only have an on-off switch, so the heat can't be adjusted.

If you choose an electric pan, be mindful that, just like a pancake griddle, different areas of the pan will get hotter and cooler—the cups that are farthest from the heating coil will not get as hot as those in the center. Once you get a sense of this, you can avoid using those parts of the pan, or you can simply cook those takoyaki a bit longer. The electric pan is a fun option if you want to cook right at the dinner table but don't have a portable butane burner. When shopping for an electric model, be sure to get one with a removable cooking surface to make clean-up easier.

Your Takoyaki Kitchen

A few tools, many of which you might already have on hand, will help you get the best results when cooking with any style of takoyaki pan.

Wooden Picks: Never use forks or other metal utensils on the cooking surface of your takoyaki pan, as they'll scratch the nonstick surface. Instead, use wooden picks to turn the takoyaki or remove them from the pan. Although you can buy special takoyaki picks, I simply use the disposable bamboo skewers sold for kebabs. They can be washed and used many times.

Chopsticks: A pair of bamboo chopsticks are good for removing cooked takoyaki from the pan. They can also be used for carefully placing pieces of the filling into the takoyaki as they cook, or to arrange the toppings from some of the recipes in this book, such as the vegetable mixture that goes on the Polenta Cups on page 56 or the seaweed that tops the Rice Cups on page 26.

Tiny Ladle: The cups in a takoyaki pan hold about 1½ tablespoons. A small ladle that holds about half an ounce is perfect for scooping and pouring thin batters, such as the traditional takoyaki batter, into the pan. You can find these ladles at restaurant supply stores or kitchen specialty stores.

Cookie Scoops: I like to use cookie scoops—the kind that look like mini ice-cream scoops and have a little spring-loaded trigger to eject the food—for scooping thicker batters, like the muffin and cake batters in this book. I recommend having two: one with a 1½-tablespoon capacity and another with a 1-tablespoon capacity.

Silicone Gripper: Many takoyaki pans don't have heatproof handles. A pair of silicone gripper mitts, just big enough to fit your fingers and thumbs, are just the right size to grip the handles of the pan.

Pastry Brush: Takoyaki chefs use a round, soft bristled brush that fits perfectly into the takoyaki pan to oil the cups. These special brushes are hard to come by in the United States, but a pastry brush will do the trick. I often just use a wadded-up paper towel.

Butane Burner: Some takoyaki pan manufacturers also sell little butane burners so that you can make takoyaki right at your dining room table. (Be sure to place a heatproof barrier underneath the pan to protect your table.)

Top 5 Takoyaki Tips and Tricks

These tips will help you become a seasoned pro at making takoyaki and other bite-sized treats in your takoyaki pan.

1. **Have all your ingredients ready to go.** Takoyaki is a pretty fast-paced food to cook; it takes only a few minutes from start to finish. Have all of your ingredients cut up and arranged next to your takoyaki pan, along with the pick and other tools you'll need. (Professional chefs call this organized arrangement *mise en place*). This way, you'll be able to work quickly and efficiently.

2. **Don't overfill.** If you're making something with a batter, make sure to fill the cups to just below the rim, since the batter will likely expand a bit as it cooks. It's unlikely the pan will overflow, as the pans have a lip to prevent spills, but you'll get a neater result if the cups are filled with just the right amount.

3. **Master the flip.** Watch carefully as your food cooks. With batter recipes, you'll be able to see the edges get dry and crisp looking, and you can use the pick to pull the ball away from the side of the pan to check the underside. To flip a takoyaki or the other batter-based recipes in this book, use a pick to poke one edge downward until the whole ball starts rotating. Let some of the batter flow back into the cup as you turn the ball. This will make it more rounded. Continue turning until the ball is completely inverted. Often the second side will take less time to cook than the first.

4. **Know how to flip delicate foods.** For more tender foods, or if something is stuck in the pan, you can use two picks. With one in each hand, push down on one side of the ball while pulling up on the other to roll the ball.

5. **Get to know your pan.** Naturally, the parts of the pan closest to the heat source will get the hottest. Whether you're using an electric pan or a stovetop pan, understanding which parts of the pan are going to get the hottest is important, as those takoyaki will cook faster than the others. Fill these cups last and check them first to make sure that you turn them and remove them before they burn. You can also move the outer pieces briefly into the hotter, inner cups to brown them a little more before they're finished cooking.

CHAPTER ONE

ASIAN
FAVORITES

Dashi

This broth, which has a neutral, subtle flavor reminiscent of the sea, is to Japanese cooking what chicken stock is in Western cuisine. It's the base of many soups, and it is the liquid used to make traditional takoyaki batter. I learned this very basic version in culinary school. The good news is that, unlike chicken stock, it takes only a few minutes to make! You can find kombu and bonito flakes at any Asian grocery store or in the international section of your local supermarket.

4 cups water

1 piece kombu (dried kelp), about 1 inch by 2 inches, rinsed

1/3 cup bonito flakes (dried shaved fish flakes)

1. Place the water and the kombu in a medium saucepan. Let sit for 15 minutes until the kombu softens.

2. Bring the pan to a boil over high heat. Just as the water begins to boil, remove the kombu and discard. Bring the water to a full boil, then remove from the heat and stir in the bonito flakes. Let sit for 5 minutes, and strain out the bonito. Refrigerate until needed, up to 5 days.

Takoyaki Fillings

Use this chart to make up your own combination of takoyaki fillings. You can set out any assortment of ingredients and invent your own takoyaki flavors!

Chopped Vegetables

Scallion

Edamame

Red bell pepper

Corn

Broccoli

Asparagus, steamed

Meat and Seafood

Ground pork, cooked

Smoked salmon, chopped or flaked

Crabmeat, cooked and shredded

Duck, cooked and shredded

Trout, cooked and shredded or chopped

Minced Garnishes

Cilantro

Thai basil

Peanuts

Mint

Fresh or pickled ginger

Chives

Wasabi

Bonito flakes

Sauces

You can buy traditional takoyaki sauce (a bit like Worcestershire sauce) at an Asian grocery store, or substitute your favorite teriyaki sauce

Japanese-style mayonnaise

TRADITIONAL OCTOPUS TAKOYAKI

If you order takoyaki in a Japanese restaurant, it'll most likely be filled with octopus, just like the original recipe developed back in the 1930s. You can buy fresh or frozen cooked octopus at an Asian supermarket or a well-stocked fishmonger. Frozen octopus is not only convenient, since you can thaw just the amount you need, but the freezing process also tenderizes the meat.

Makes 16 pieces

1 egg
1 cup dashi broth (see recipe, page 16)
¾ cup all-purpose flour
Vegetable oil, as needed
4 ounces octopus, chopped and cooked
2 scallions, finely chopped
2 tablespoons pickled ginger, finely chopped
Takoyaki sauce or teriyaki sauce, for serving
Japanese-style mayonnaise, for serving
¼ cup bonito flakes, for serving

1. In a medium mixing bowl, beat the egg until smooth. Whisk in the broth, then the flour. Continue whisking until well combined and no lumps remain.

2. Brush the cups of the takoyaki pan with vegetable oil, and heat the pan over medium heat. Using a tablespoon or a small ladle, spoon the batter into the cups of the heated takoyaki pan until they are just barely full. Drop a small amount of octopus, scallion, and ginger into each cup. Let cook for about 4 minutes, until the edges start looking

cooked. Using a pick, carefully rotate each takoyaki
halfway, letting the raw batter flow into the pan, and then
rotate all of the way so that the other side cooks. Cook for
an additional 3 to 4 minutes until evenly browned.

3. Remove the takoyaki from the pan using two picks or
chopsticks. Drizzle with takoyaki sauce and mayonnaise,
sprinkle with bonito flakes, and serve immediately.

Note: *If you're starting with raw octopus, cut it into small
chunks with a sharp knife and simmer them in water or
dashi for about 15 to 20 minutes, until tender.*

SHRIMP AND SCALLION TAKOYAKI

If you can't find octopus in your area, or if you simply want a change from a traditional takoyaki, shrimp makes a good stand-in (and is a good use of leftover cooked shrimp from a previous meal). You can use cooked shrimp, or simply poach raw shrimp in simmering water for about 3 minutes, until they're pink and opaque.

Makes 16

1 egg

1 cup dashi broth (see recipe, page 16)

¾ cup all-purpose flour

Vegetable oil, as needed

4 ounces shrimp, cooked and chopped

2 scallions, finely chopped

2 tablespoons minced cilantro

Takoyaki sauce or teriyaki sauce, for serving

Japanese-style mayonnaise, for serving

¼ cup bonito flakes, for serving

1. In a medium mixing bowl, beat the egg until smooth. Whisk in the broth, then the flour, and whisk until well combined and no lumps remain.

2. Brush the cups of the takoyaki pan with vegetable oil, and heat the pan over medium heat. Using a tablespoon or a small ladle, spoon the batter into the cups of the heated takoyaki pan until they are just barely full. Drop a small amount of shrimp, scallion, and cilantro into each cup. Let cook for about 4 minutes, until the edges start looking cooked. Using a pick, carefully rotate each

takoyaki halfway, letting the raw batter flow into the
pan, and then rotate all of the way so that the other side
cooks. Cook for an additional 3 to 4 minutes until evenly
browned.

3. Remove the takoyaki from the pan using two picks or
chopsticks. Drizzle with takoyaki sauce and mayonnaise,
sprinkle with bonito flakes, and serve immediately.

SHIITAKE AND LEEK TAKOYAKI

Chewy, meaty mushrooms stand in for seafood in this vegetarian version of takoyaki, and the miso broth adds a mellow note to the batter. Instead of the bonito flakes, try crisp tempura flakes, which look a bit like crisped rice cereal but are basically crunchy crumbs made of fried batter.

Makes 16

1 tablespoon vegetable oil, plus more as needed

1/2 cup leek, white part only, diced

2 cups chopped, stemmed shiitake mushrooms

Kosher salt

1 tablespoon white miso paste

1 1/4 cups warm water

1 egg

3/4 cup all-purpose flour

Takoyaki sauce or teriyaki sauce, for serving

Japanese-style mayonnaise, for serving

1/4 cup tempura flakes, for serving

1. Heat 1 tablespoon vegetable oil in a medium nonstick skillet over medium heat. Add the leek and mushrooms and sauté, stirring occasionally, until the mushrooms soften and the leek is translucent, about 5 minutes. Season to taste with salt, set aside.

2. In a measuring cup, combine the miso paste and water to form a broth. In a medium mixing bowl, beat the egg until smooth. Whisk in the broth, then the flour. Continue whisking until well combined and no lumps remain.

3. Brush the cups of the takoyaki pan with vegetable oil and heat the pan over medium heat. Using a tablespoon or a small ladle, spoon the batter into the cups of the heated takoyaki pan until they are just barely full. Drop a small amount of the leek-mushroom mixture into each cup. Let cook for about 4 minutes, until the edges start looking cooked. Using a pick, carefully rotate each takoyaki halfway, letting the raw batter flow into the pan, and then rotate all of the way so that the other side cooks. Cook for an additional 3 to 4 minutes until evenly browned.

4. Remove the takoyaki from the pan using picks or chopsticks. Drizzled with takoyaki sauce and mayonnaise, sprinkle with tempura flakes, and serve immediately.

GRILLED SALMON ONIGIRI

One of my husband's favorite dishes at our local sushi restaurant is the onigiri. This rice treat comes in a big triangle, belted with a strip of seaweed. The rice exterior is crisp and toasty, and the inside is filled with flavorful salmon skin. I developed this recipe for him, but my kids love it, too. I made extras thinking it would be great for their lunches, but when I went to pack them, it turns out they'd snacked on the entire batch!

Makes about 24

1½ cups short-grained white Japanese rice, e.g., Nishiki

1 teaspoon fine sea salt

3 ounces hot-smoked salmon

Vegetable oil, as needed

2 sheets nori paper, cut into twenty-four ½-inch strips

Ponzu sauce, for serving

1. Place the rice in a medium saucepan and cover with water. Rub the grains together in your fist, then drain the water off. Repeat several times until water is no longer cloudy. Drain as much water as you can, then add 1½ cups fresh water to the pan, brushing down any grains stuck to the sides of the pan. Bring to a simmer over medium-high heat, then cover and reduce heat to just maintain a simmer. Cook for 15 minutes, then turn off the heat and let sit, covered, for an additional 10 minutes. Rice should be firm but cooked all the way through.

2. When the rice is cool enough to handle, fill a shallow bowl with water. Wet your hands with the water, and scoop a bit of rice into your palm. Flatten the rice slightly

with your thumb, and put a few flakes of salmon in the middle. Pack the rice around the salmon, as if you were making a snowball. Make the ball about the same size as the cups in your takoyaki pan. Continue making salmon-filled rice balls, wetting your hands occasionally to keep the rice from sticking.

3. Brush the cups of the takoyaki pan with vegetable oil and heat the pan over medium heat. Put the onigiri balls into the cups and let cook for about 4 minutes, until the underside is lightly toasted and crispy. Use a pick to turn the balls over, and cook the other side for 3 to 4 minutes. Remove the balls from the pan to a platter, and cook the remaining onigiri. Wrap each ball with a piece of nori, wetting the end of the strip to stick it to itself. Serve warm or at room temperature. Onigiri will keep, covered and refrigerated, for 1 to 2 days, although the rice might get a bit hard.

RICE CUPS WITH SEAWEED AND TOBIKO

Some say the best part of a bowl of rice is the crispy bit at the bottom, where it's toasted and crunchy, rather than fluffy and tender. That's what gives the Korean rice dish bibimbap, traditionally made in a screaming-hot stone bowl, its appeal. It's also a sought-after morsel in a pan of paella. In this recipe, cooked rice is toasted into little cups just the right size to hold a bite-sized burst of flavor. Look for tobiko (flying fish roe) and seaweed salad at an international or Asian grocery store, or ask your local sushi restaurant if they'd consider selling some to you.

Makes about 45

1½ cups short-grained white Japanese rice, e.g., Nishiki

2 tablespoons rice vinegar

½ teaspoon fine sea salt

½ teaspoon granulated sugar

Vegetable oil, as needed

¼ cup fresh seaweed salad

1 ounce tobiko (flying fish roe)

1. Place the rice in a medium saucepan and cover with water. Rub the grains together in your fist, then drain the water off. Repeat several times until water is no longer cloudy. Drain as much water as you can, then add 1½ cups fresh water to the pan, brushing down any grains stuck to the sides of the pan. Bring to a simmer over medium-high heat, then cover and reduce heat to just maintain a simmer. Cook for 15 minutes, then turn off the heat and let sit, covered, for an additional 10 minutes. Rice should be firm but cooked all the way through.

2. Sprinkle the rice with rice vinegar, sea salt, and sugar, and use a flat spatula to stir the ingredients into the rice.

3. Brush the cups of the takoyaki pan with vegetable oil and heat the pan over medium heat. Using a small cookie scoop or a tablespoon, drop scoops of rice, measuring about 1 tablespoon each, into the takoyaki cups. Use the back of a teaspoon to press down the rice in the center, squishing it up along the sides of each cup, to form a shallow bowl in the rice. Let cook until the undersides are crisp and lightly browned, checking the first rice cup you formed after around 5 to 7 minutes. Remove from the takoyaki pan using two picks or chopsticks, and let cool on a platter.

4. When the rice cups are cool, fill each one with a little seaweed salad (I found it helpful to use chopsticks to pick up a few strands of seaweed and arrange them in the cups), and top with a small scoop of tobiko, around ¼ teaspoon. Serve at room temperature.

Note: *This recipe is also delicious when made with larger salmon roe, although they're much pricier than the flying fish roe. Once you've mastered these little cups, you can fill them with anything you can imagine: a flake of smoked salmon and a tiny sprig of dill, or a few pieces of diced cucumber and a piece of pickled ginger.*

CRAB RANGOON DUMPLINGS

I've always loved these creamy, crab-filled dumplings at Chinese restaurants but often wondered about their origin. Cream cheese doesn't seem to be a particularly authentic Asian ingredient. Indeed, a little sleuthing revealed that crab Rangoon is credited to the Polynesian restaurant chain Trader Vic's, which had these little dumplings on the menu as early as the 1950s. They're easy enough to make at home, and they are fun cocktail-party fare, especially for a retro- or tiki-themed soiree.

Makes 16

4 ounces reduced-fat cream cheese, softened

½ cup chopped imitation crab

1 scallion, minced

1 teaspoon soy sauce

16 round gyoza wrappers

Vegetable oil, as needed

Sweet chili sauce, for serving

1. In a small bowl, combine the cream cheese, crab, scallion, and soy sauce. Mash together with a spoon until all the ingredients are well mixed.

2. Fill a small dish with water. On a clean work surface, lay out a few gyoza wrappers. Place 1 scant teaspoon of the cream cheese mixture in the center of each wrapper. Use your finger to wet the edges of the wrappers, then bunch up the edges into the middle to form a pouch. Press together to seal. Repeat with the remaining ingredients.

3. Brush the cups of the takoyaki pan with vegetable oil and heat the pan over medium heat. Place the dumplings into each cup of the takoyaki pan, pressing down lightly to make sure the bottoms of the dumplings make contact with the bottom of the cups. Cook for 3 minutes. While the dumplings are cooking, brush the tops of the dumplings lightly with vegetable oil. When the undersides of the dumplings are crisp and brown, turn each over and cook for 2 to 3 minutes more, until equally browned. Remove from pan. Let cool slightly, and serve with sweet chili sauce for dipping.

GINGER-TOFU POT STICKERS

Dumplings are fun and easy to make, and this vegetarian filling has universal appeal, whether you eat meat or not. It's also a great recipe to prepare as a side for an Asian noodle soup or to make ahead and pack in a lunchbox—they're even tasty cold! If you're entertaining, I like the idea of having a dumpling party and using a variety of fillings. Guests can assemble their own dumplings and cook them in the takoyaki pan.

Makes 18 to 20

2 teaspoons sesame oil

2 scallions, minced

2 teaspoons minced ginger

2 cups shredded coleslaw mix (cabbage and carrot blend)

2 ounces firm tofu

1 tablespoon soy sauce

1 tablespoon rice vinegar

1/4 teaspoon kosher salt

1/8 teaspoon white pepper

20 gyoza or pot-sticker wrappers

Vegetable oil, as needed

Ponzu sauce, for serving

1. In a medium nonstick skillet, heat sesame oil over medium heat. Add the scallions and sauté until softened, about 3 minutes. Add the ginger and cook for 1 minute, stirring constantly. Add the coleslaw mix and sauté for 4 to 5 minutes, stirring frequently, until soft. Crumble the tofu into the pan and stir in the soy sauce and rice

vinegar. Cook, stirring frequently, for 2 minutes more to integrate the flavors. Season with salt and pepper, transfer to a bowl, and let cool.

2. Fill a small dish with water. Lay a few dumpling wrappers on a clean work surface. Place 1 scant teaspoon of the coleslaw mixture in the center of each wrapper. Use your finger to wet the edges of the wrappers, then bunch up the edges into the middle to form a pouch. Press together to seal. Repeat with the remaining ingredients.

3. Brush the cups of the takoyaki pan with vegetable oil and heat the pan over medium heat. Place the dumplings into each cup of the takoyaki pan, pressing down lightly to make sure the bottoms of the dumplings make contact with the bottom of the cups. Cook for about 4 minutes. While the dumplings are cooking, brush the tops of the dumplings lightly with vegetable oil. When the undersides of the dumplings are crisp and brown, turn each over and cook for 3 to 4 minutes more, until equally browned. Remove from pan. Serve warm with ponzu sauce for dipping.

CHAPTER TWO

BREAKFAST BITES

PANCAKE AND SAUSAGE POPS

These pops are so much more fun to eat than regular pancakes! They're just the thing to grab and go on a busy morning or to serve at brunch. While I love the sweet-and-savory contrast with the sausage, you could also drop a few blueberries or banana pieces into the batter instead if you want an all-sweet treat.

Makes about 32

2 eggs

$^1/_2$ cup whole or low-fat milk

$^1/_2$ cup buttermilk

6 tablespoons butter, melted and cooled, divided

$1^1/_3$ cups all-purpose flour

2 teaspoons baking powder

$^1/_2$ teaspoon kosher salt

6 ounces cooked sausage, cut into $^3/_4$-inch chunks

1 tablespoon maple syrup

1. In a mixing bowl, whisk the eggs. Whisk in the milk, buttermilk, and 4 tablespoons butter. In a separate bowl, stir together the flour, baking powder, and salt. Mix the dry ingredients into the wet ingredients, and whisk until very few lumps remain.

2. Brush the cups of the takoyaki pan with the rest of the melted butter and heat the pan over medium heat. Drop a piece of sausage into each cup. Using a cookie scoop, fill the cups with batter until they are just barely full. Let

cook for 2 to 3 minutes, until the edges begin to set and the underside is lightly browned. Use a pick to partially turn each pancake pop, letting the batter flow into the pan, and then turn each over completely. Cook for 1 to 2 minutes more, until the sides are evenly browned. Remove from the pan using two picks or chopsticks, and serve warm with maple syrup for dipping.

BLUEBERRY MUFFIN BALLS

These treats are a snap to whip up for breakfast—they cook much more quickly than regular muffins, and the tangy-sweet glaze makes them even more appealing.

Makes about 48

For the muffin balls:

1⅓ cups all-purpose flour

½ cup granulated sugar

¾ teaspoon salt

2 teaspoons baking powder

2 eggs

1 cup whole milk

1 stick unsalted butter, melted and cooled, plus more as needed

½ cup blueberries (frozen is fine)

For the glaze:

½ cup powdered sugar

2 teaspoons freshly squeezed lemon juice

1 teaspoon water

1. In a medium mixing bowl, combine the flour, sugar, salt, and baking powder. Use a whisk or fork to mix the dry ingredients completely. In another medium bowl, whisk the eggs, then whisk in the milk and butter. Stir the dry ingredients into the wet ingredients.

2. Brush the cups of the takoyaki pan with melted butter, and heat pan over medium-low heat. Fill each cup with about 1 tablespoon batter, using a spoon or a small

cookie scoop, and drop two or three blueberries in each cup, poking them in to mostly submerge them in the batter. Let cook for 4 to 5 minutes, until the underside is browned, then turn each ball over with a pick and cook for 3 to 4 minutes more, until they are evenly browned. Remove each from the pan using two picks or chopsticks, and let cool slightly.

3. While the muffins are cooling, make the glaze. In a small bowl, stir together the powdered sugar, lemon juice, and water to make a thick, smooth glaze. While the muffins are still a little warm, dip the top of each one in the glaze, and let cool until set. Serve warm or at room temperature.

STUFFED FRENCH TOAST

Set out a bunch of jars of jam and a block of cream cheese, and everyone can make their own stuffed French toast bites with their favorite jams. While raspberry is my favorite for this recipe, I also love using orange marmalade or cherry preserves.

Makes 12

2 tablespoons cream cheese

4 slices white bread

2 tablespoons raspberry jam

2 eggs

2 tablespoons half-and-half

1 teaspoon maple syrup

1/2 teaspoon ground cinnamon

1 teaspoon vanilla extract

2 tablespoons butter, melted

Maple syrup, for serving

1. Spread a tablespoon of cream cheese each on two pieces of bread, and a tablespoon of jam each on the remaining two pieces of bread. Sandwich together the cream cheese bread with the jam bread to make two sandwiches. Using a 1½-inch round cookie cutter, cut out six circles from each sandwich.

2. In a medium mixing bowl, whisk the eggs with a fork. Whisk in the half-and-half, maple syrup, cinnamon, and vanilla extract.

3. Brush the cups of the takoyaki pan with melted butter and heat the pan over medium heat. Working with two or three at a time, dip the bread rounds into the egg mixture, turning them over and letting them soak up the batter for a moment, then transfer them to the heated takoyaki pan. Cook the French toast about 3 minutes, until the underside is browned, then use a pick to turn them over and cook for 2 to 3 minutes more, until evenly browned. Use chopsticks or two picks to remove the French toast from the pan, and let cool slightly before serving. Serve with maple syrup for dipping.

MINI OMELET PUFFS

At your next brunch, set up a takoyaki pan and an assortment of toppings, and let guests make their own little omelet puffs. These are like a cross between an omelet and a soufflé, with an airy, puffy interior and a lightly browned exterior.

Makes 16 to 18

3 eggs
1 tablespoon half-and-half or heavy cream
1/8 teaspoon kosher salt
1/8 teaspoon black pepper
Vegetable oil, as needed

Topping options: finely grated cheese, such as sharp cheddar; minced red bell pepper; minced ham; finely chopped broccoli; thinly sliced green onion; flaked smoked trout; bacon bits; cooked, minced mushrooms

1. In a medium mixing bowl, whisk together the eggs, half-and-half, salt, and pepper.

2. Brush the cups of the takoyaki pan with vegetable oil and heat the pan over medium heat. Using a ladle or a spoon, spoon about 1 tablespoon of egg mixture into each cup, and immediately sprinkle with any combination of the fillings. Once the edges of the omelets begin to set and the underside is lightly browned, about 2 minutes, use wooden picks to turn the omelets over. Cook for 1 to 2 minutes more until the other side is evenly browned. Remove from the pan using two picks or chopsticks, and serve warm.

CHAPTER THREE

SAVORY
SNACKS

ARANCINI (RISOTTO BALLS)

Crispy-on-the-outside, creamy-on-the-inside arancini are one of my favorite treats to order at an Italian restaurant. Really, they're Italy's answer to takoyaki, so it makes sense that they can be made in your takoyaki pan. Making classic risotto from scratch is a little time intensive, but it's worth the effort for the result, and it can certainly be done while you're doing other things in the kitchen.

Makes about 20

3 cups chicken or vegetable stock

Pinch saffron, optional

1 tablespoon extra virgin olive oil

1 medium shallot, minced

1 cup risotto rice (also called *Arborio rice*)

¼ cup white wine

Kosher salt

¾ cup finely grated parmesan cheese

Freshly ground white pepper

Vegetable oil, as needed

3 ounces mozzarella cheese, cut into ½-inch cubes

1. In a medium saucepan, heat the stock over medium-low heat. Keep warm on the back of your stove. If using, add the saffron to the stock and stir to combine.

2. In another medium saucepan, preferably one with rounded sides (called a *saucier*), heat the olive oil over medium heat. Reduce the heat to medium-low, add the shallot and sauté, stirring, until the shallot is soft and translucent, about 3 to 4 minutes. Add the risotto and toast, stirring constantly, for 1 minute or until the rice smells nutty.

3. Add the white wine and stir, scraping up any browned bits from the bottom of the pan. Season lightly with salt. Cook, stirring occasionally, until the wine has been completely absorbed.

4. Begin stirring in the broth, about ½ cup at a time, waiting until the liquid has been mostly absorbed before adding the next amount. Stir occasionally, and be sure to scrap stray bits of rice down from the sides of the pan.

5. When all the stock has been added, cook, stirring occasionally, until the rice has a firm texture but is not at all crunchy. Stir in the parmesan cheese until melted, and season to taste with salt and pepper.

6. Spray an 8-inch-square baking dish with cooking spray. Spoon the risotto into the dish. Let cool, then refrigerate until firm, at least 2 hours.

7. When the risotto is cool and set, brush the cups of the takoyaki pan with vegetable oil and heat the pan over medium heat. Using a medium-sized cookie scoop, scoop up enough risotto to fill the scoop about two-thirds full, then press a cheese cube into the middle. Scoop up a little more risotto to cover the cheese, and drop into one of the cups in the pan. The risotto should mound up out of the cup. Continue forming these balls. After the first ball becomes crisp and browned on the underside, about 3 to 4 minutes, carefully turn it over with a wooden pick and cook the other side for an additional 3 to 4 minutes, until evenly browned. Use two picks or chopsticks to remove each ball as they finish. Eat warm or at room temperature. Balls can be made ahead of time, cooled and refrigerated for up to 2 days. To reheat, place them on a baking sheet sprayed with cooking spray and bake in a 325°F oven until heated through, about 15 minutes.

Note: *Don't have white wine? Dry vermouth is a handy substitute for it, in the same quantity. Or use 2 tablespoons white wine vinegar or apple cider vinegar combined with 2 tablespoons water.*

CHEESY HASH BROWN BITES

Packaged shredded hash brown potatoes are a super-convenient ingredient to have stashed in your freezer, if only because it means you can whip up these nuggets on a whim. They're just as good alongside eggs at breakfast as they are as a late-night snack.

Makes 20

4 cups frozen, shredded hash brown potatoes

1 1/2 teaspoons dried minced onion

1/4 teaspoon kosher salt

1/8 teaspoon freshly ground black pepper

Vegetable oil, as needed

1/3 cup grated sharp cheddar cheese

1/4 cup bacon bits

1. Cook the hash browns in a medium nonstick skillet over medium-low heat, stirring and turning frequently, for 3 to 4 minutes until the potatoes are soft and thawed but not browned.

2. Transfer the potatoes to a medium bowl and combine with the onion, salt, and pepper. Toss to distribute seasonings.

3. Brush the cups of the takoyaki pan with vegetable oil and heat the pan over medium heat. Spoon about 1 tablespoon of the potato mixture into each cup, pushing down slightly to compress. Top each with a pinch of cheese and a few bacon bits. Cover with about ½ tablespoon more potato. Let cook for 5 to 6 minutes, until the underside is crusty and browned. Using a pick, turn each Hash Brown Bite over in the pan and cook 3 to 4 minutes more, until the other side is evenly browned. Remove from the pan using two picks or chopsticks and let cool slightly before serving warm.

Note: *For the best results, look for real bacon bits or crumbled bacon in shelf-stable packaging, rather than artificial bacon bits. You can also fry up two pieces of bacon until crisp. Let them cool and crumble them into small pieces.*

PIGS IN A PUFF

Perfect for a game-day snack or a kids' party, this is a delicious variation on pigs in a blanket. You can use regular dill pickle spears, but the baby dill pickles, called *gherkins*, have a really nice crunch to them that stands up even when cooked.

Makes 16

¼ cup all-purpose flour

½ teaspoon kosher salt

1 teaspoon baking powder

1 egg

½ cup whole milk

Vegetable oil, as needed

2 hot dogs, halved lengthwise and cut into ¼-inch pieces

¼ cup diced baby dill pickles

Yellow mustard or grainy mustard, for serving

1. In a small bowl, use a fork to combine the flour, salt, and baking powder. In a medium mixing bowl, whisk the egg and stir in the milk. Stir the dry ingredients into the wet, and whisk to form a smooth batter. It will be relatively thin.

2. Brush the cups of the takoyaki pan with vegetable oil and heat the pan over medium heat. Place two hot dog pieces and a few pieces of pickle in each cup. Immediately fill each cup with about 1 tablespoon batter, just enough to fill the cups. Let cook for about 3 minutes, until the edges start to firm up and the undersides are lightly browned. Use a pick to turn over each ball, tucking any overflowing bits into the cup with the pick. Let cook about 3 minutes more, until evenly browned. Remove from the pan using two picks or chopsticks, and serve warm or at room temperature with mustard for dipping.

JALAPEÑO CORNBREAD BALLS

Next time you make chili, serve it with a basket of these spicy nuggets that have a cheesy surprise in the inside. While they're delicious warm, when the cheese is still gooey, they're just as tasty at room temperature. I like to pack a few in my lunch to go with a thermos of soup.

Makes 48

1¼ cups all-purpose flour

¾ cup cornmeal

2 tablespoons brown sugar

2 teaspoons baking powder

1 teaspoon kosher salt

2 eggs

1 cup whole milk

1 stick butter, melted and cooled

⅓ cup diced jarred jalapeño, drained

Vegetable oil, as needed

4 ounces pepper jack cheese, cut into ¼-inch cubes

1. In a medium mixing bowl, combine the flour, cornmeal, brown sugar, baking powder, and salt. Use a whisk or a fork to mix the dry ingredients completely. In another medium bowl, whisk the eggs, then whisk in the milk and the cooled butter. Stir the dry ingredients into the wet ingredients. Fold in the jalapeños.

2. Brush the cups of the takoyaki pan with vegetable oil, and heat the pan over medium-low heat. Fill each cup with about 1 tablespoon batter, using a spoon or a small cookie scoop, and drop 1 or 2 pieces of cheese into the middle of each, and press the cheese into the batter so that it is mostly submerged. Let cook for about 4 minutes, until the underside is browned, then turn each ball over with a pick and cook for 3 to 4 minutes more, until they are evenly browned. Remove each from the pan using two picks or chopsticks. Serve warm or at room temperature.

BUFFALO CHICKEN TAKOYAKI

My husband is a fan of all things buffalo, so I developed this recipe just for him. It's a fun riff on a classic for the big game, or it makes a yummy accompaniment to a bowl of soup or a salad.

Makes 16

1 egg

1 cup water

1 tablespoon buffalo sauce, such as Frank's RedHot, plus more for serving

3/4 cup all-purpose flour

Vegetable oil, as needed

4 ounces cooked chicken breast, diced

1 celery rib, diced

2 ounces crumbled blue cheese

Blue cheese dressing, for serving

1. In a medium mixing bowl, beat the egg until smooth. Whisk in the water and buffalo sauce, then the flour, and whisk until well combined and no lumps remain.

2. Brush the cups of the takoyaki pan with vegetable oil and heat the pan over medium heat. Using a tablespoon or a small ladle, spoon the batter into the cups of the heated takoyaki pan until they are just barely full. Drop a couple pieces of chicken, celery, and blue cheese into each cup. Let cook for about 3 minutes, until the edges start to look cooked. Using a pick, carefully rotate each takoyaki halfway, letting the raw batter flow into the pan, and then

rotate all of the way so that the other side cooks. Cook for an additional 2 to 3 minutes until evenly browned.

3. Remove the takoyaki from the pan using two picks or chopsticks, drizzle with additional buffalo sauce and blue cheese dressing, and serve immediately.

ROOT VEGETABLE FRITTERS WITH HORSERADISH CREAM

These hearty nuggets are perfect to make in the fall or winter, when root vegetables such as sweet potatoes, beets, and turnips are at their peak. Red beets will give these balls a dramatic ruby hue, but you can also use yellow beets, which won't stain your fingers quite as much.

Makes 24 to 26

For the sauce:

1/2 cup low-fat sour cream

2 teaspoons prepared horseradish

1/4 teaspoon kosher salt

1/4 teaspoon smoked paprika

For the fritters:

1 small sweet potato, peeled

1 medium parsnip, peeled

1 medium beet, peeled

1 medium carrot, peeled

1/2 medium sweet onion

1/3 cup breadcrumbs

1 teaspoon baking powder

1/2 teaspoon kosher salt

1/8 teaspoon freshly ground black pepper

1 egg

Vegetable oil, as needed

1. In a small bowl, combine the sour cream, horseradish, salt, and paprika. Set aside.

2. Grate each of the vegetables and combine in a medium bowl. You should have about 3 cups of grated vegetables. Sprinkle with the breadcrumbs, baking powder, salt, and pepper, and toss to coat.

3. In a small bowl, whisk the egg. Pour the egg over the vegetable mixture, and stir to combine thoroughly.

4. Brush the cups of the takoyaki pan with vegetable oil and heat the pan over medium heat. Using a tablespoon or a small ladle, spoon the vegetable mixture into the cups of the pan. They should mound over the top but not overflow too much. Cook for about 4 minutes, until the underside has formed a browned crust. Use two picks to turn each ball over, tucking any loose bits into the cups. Cook for 4 to 5 minutes more, until evenly browned. Remove from the pan using two picks or chopsticks, and serve warm with the horseradish cream for dipping.

POLENTA CUPS WITH SAUTÉED VEGETABLES

Here's a great use for leftover polenta: spread it thinly on a baking sheet and chill it until firm, then cut out rounds to sear in your takoyaki pan and use as little vessels for a savory veggie mixture. Or you could use one of my favorite kitchen shortcuts: a tube of prepared polenta. Slicing the cylinder on the diagonal to create long "surfboards" will give you more surface space to cut out the little circles.

Makes 24

- ½ tablespoon extra virgin olive oil
- ½ cup diced red onion (about ½ onion)
- ½ cup diced red bell pepper (about ½ medium)
- 1 small zucchini, grated
- ¼ teaspoon kosher salt
- ⅛ teaspoon freshly ground black pepper
- 1 one-pound tube prepared polenta
- Vegetable oil, as needed
- ¼ cup grated parmesan cheese (about 1 ounce)

1. In a medium nonstick skillet, heat the olive oil over medium heat. Add the onion and bell pepper and sauté, stirring occasionally, until soft and the onion is translucent, about 3 to 4 minutes. Add the zucchini and salt and sauté for 2 to 3 minutes until the zucchini is soft and any water that was released has cooked off. Cover the pan to keep warm and set aside.

2. Slice the polenta on the diagonal into ½-inch thick pieces. Use a 1½-inch round cookie cutter to cut out rounds from

the polenta. Brush the cups of the takoyaki pan with vegetable oil and heat the pan over medium heat. Place each polenta round into a cup of the takoyaki pan, and let cook for about 2 minutes to soften the polenta. Use two picks or chopsticks to flip over the polenta, and use the blunt handle of a kitchen utensil (or a tart tamper if you have one), to gently push the polenta into the bowl shape of the takoyaki cups. Let cook for 3 to 4 minutes until the underside has developed a browned crust. Use chopsticks or picks to remove the polenta cups from the pan.

3. Use chopsticks or a small fork to fill each cup with a little of the vegetable filling, about 1 teaspoon. Sprinkle the top of each with parmesan cheese, and serve warm.

Note: *You can gather the scraps of polenta left over from cutting out the rounds and warm them in a bowl in the microwave until soft. Then you can spread out the polenta in a pan, let it firm up, and cut out even more rounds.*

MAC & CHEESE BITES

If you're a fan of the crispy, crunchy top of a big pan of macaroni and cheese, these bite-sized morsels are for you. They start with the easiest-ever recipe for mac and cheese, and then they quickly fry up into fritters in your takoyaki pan for a fun party food or afternoon snack.

Makes about 24

1³/₄ cups whole milk
1¹/₂ cups elbow macaroni
1 teaspoon Dijon mustard
1 cup grated extra-sharp cheddar cheese (about 4 ounces)
Kosher salt
Freshly ground black pepper
Vegetable oil, as needed
¹/₂ cup breadcrumbs

1. In a medium saucepan, bring milk to a simmer over medium-high heat. Add the pasta and cook according to the time indicated on the package, usually around 9 minutes. Stir frequently to prevent the pasta from sticking to the bottom of the pan.

2. When the pasta is cooked al dente (firm but cooked through), turn off the heat. There should still be a little milk left in the bottom of the pan. Add the mustard and cheese, and stir until the cheese is melted and mixed with the milk to make a smooth sauce. Season to taste with salt and pepper.

3. Spoon the mac and cheese into a greased 8-inch square baking pan, making a layer about 1 inch thick, even if the macaroni doesn't cover the whole bottom of the pan. Let cool until firm, at least an hour.

4. When the mac and cheese is cool and set, brush the cups of the takoyaki pan with vegetable oil and heat the pan over medium heat. Put the breadcrumbs into a shallow bowl. Use a spoon to scoop up an intact chunk of mac and cheese. Roll it carefully in the breadcrumbs, then drop it into one of the takoyaki cups. Continue filling the cups. Let the bites cook for 2 to 3 minutes, until the exterior begins to brown, then carefully turn over with a pick. Cook for 2 to 3 minutes more until evenly browned on both sides, and remove from the pan using two picks or chopsticks. Serve warm.

CHEESEBURGER MEATBALLS

With a center of gooey American cheese and a glaze of ketchup and mustard, these tasty meatballs have everything you love about a real, all-American burger. They're great on their own, but you could also put them on slider buns or serve them on a skewer with a bit of lettuce and a slice of Roma tomato.

Makes about 20

1/3 cup ketchup

1 teaspoon Dijon mustard

4 slices American cheese

1 tablespoon vegetable oil, plus more as needed

1/2 cup minced yellow onion

1 pound lean ground beef

1 egg

1/3 cup breadcrumbs

1 teaspoon kosher salt

1/2 teaspoon garlic powder

1/8 teaspoon freshly ground black pepper

1. In a small bowl, stir together the ketchup and mustard. Set aside. Unwrap the American cheese and stack it. Cut the stack of cheese into cubes, about 1/3 inch square. Set aside.

2. In a small nonstick skillet, heat 1 tablespoon vegetable oil over medium heat. Add the onion and sauté, stirring frequently, until the onion is soft and translucent, about 4 to 5 minutes. Remove from the pan to a small bowl, let cool.

3. In a medium bowl, combine the beef, egg, cooled onion, breadcrumbs, salt, garlic powder, and pepper. Use a spatula or your hands to mix all the ingredients well. Scoop up a bit of the meat mixture into your hand. Press your thumb into the middle to make an indentation, and put a chunk of cheese in the middle. Form the mixture into a ball around the cheese, making sure each ball is sized to fit into the cups of your takoyaki pan. Repeat with the remaining cheese and meat mixture.

4. Brush the cups of the takoyaki pan with vegetable oil and heat the pan over medium heat. Place a meatball into each cup. Brush the tops of the meatball with the ketchup mixture and let cook for 4 to 5 minutes, until the underside is browned. Using a pick, turn the meatballs over and brush the other side with the ketchup mixture. Let cook for another 4 to 5 minutes, or until the internal temperature of the meatballs is 165°F when checked with a meat thermometer. Serve hot or warm.

CHAPTER FOUR

DESSERTS

DESSERT TAKOYAKI

The sweet batter in this recipe puffs up around chewy dried fruit and creamy chocolate for a delicious sweet treat that's best eaten as fast as you can make it. Use this recipe as a springboard for your own dessert takoyaki combinations. A few flavors to consider: dried pineapple and cashews, candied ginger and dark chocolate, coconut flakes and dried cranberries, or mini marshmallows and milk chocolate chips.

Makes 16

1 cup warm water

2 tablespoons granulated sugar

1 egg

1 teaspoon vanilla extract

³/₄ cup all-purpose flour

Vegetable oil, as needed

¹/₄ cup dried cherries

¹/₄ cup semisweet chocolate chips

Powdered sugar, for serving (optional)

1. In a medium mixing bowl, stir together the water and the granulated sugar. Let dissolve completely. Whisk in the egg with a fork until smooth. Stir in the vanilla extract. Add the flour, and stir with the fork until no lumps remain.

2. Brush the cups of the takoyaki pan with vegetable oil and heat the pan over medium heat. Using a tablespoon or a small ladle, spoon the batter into the cups of the heated takoyaki pan, until the cups are just barely full. Drop a couple pieces of dried cherry and chocolate chips into each cup. Cook for about 4 minutes, until the edges start to look done. Using a pick, carefully rotate each takoyaki halfway, letting the raw batter flow into the pan, and then finish rotating all of the way so that the other side cooks. Cook for an additional 3 to 4 minutes until evenly browned. Using two picks or chopsticks, remove from the pan, and let cool slightly. Just before eating, dust with powdered sugar if desired.

MATCHA CAKE POPS

Green tea, with its slightly bitter, earthy taste, is a sophisticated flavor for desserts. Here, it elevates cake pops, a kids' favorite, into a much more grown-up treat. Matcha is the name for a special kind of green tea leaves that are ground into a powder and then whisked into hot water to make a beverage. Be sure to use matcha (and not green tea bags or loose green tea leaves) in this recipe.

Makes 20 to 22

1 stick butter (8 tablespoons), softened

½ cup granulated sugar

½ teaspoon salt

2 eggs, room temperature

1 teaspoon vanilla extract

2 teaspoons plus 1 tablespoon matcha powder, divided

1 cup all-purpose flour

2 tablespoons melted butter

1½ cups white chocolate chips or white candy melts

1. In the bowl of a standing mixer, beat the butter until soft, about 1 minute. Add the sugar and salt, and beat 2 to 3 minutes more on a medium-high speed, until the mixture is light and fluffy. Slow the mixer speed to add the eggs one at a time, beating completely between additions. Add the vanilla extract and 2 teaspoons of the matcha powder. Slow the mixer to a low speed, add the flour, and beat just until the flour is incorporated into a smooth batter.

2. Brush the cups of the takoyaki pan with melted butter and heat the pan over medium-low heat. Using a small cookie scoop, drop batter into each takoyaki cup, filling about two-thirds full. Let cook for 8 to 10 minutes, turn

over with a pick, and cook for 4 to 5 minutes more, until the pops are evenly browned. Using two picks or chopsticks, remove from the pan and let cool on a plate.

3. Place the white chocolate chips in a microwave-proof bowl and microwave it at half-power, in 30-second increments, stirring occasionally. When the chips are completely melted, stir in the remaining 1 tablespoon of matcha powder. Line a tray or plate with wax paper. Poke a lollipop stick or skewer into each cake pop. Holding the pops by the stick, roll each in the white chocolate, using a spoon to coat the pop completely with melted chocolate. Hold the pop over the bowl to let excess drip off, then transfer it to the wax paper–lined tray or plate. Refrigerate until the coating has hardened.

MOLTEN BROWNIE BITES

My daughter proclaimed these "illegally delicious," and she's not wrong. A few chocolate chips pushed into a simple brownie batter create a gooey center that stays soft even when the bites are cool. I like the richness of semisweet chocolate, but milk chocolate can be used too; peanut butter chips are another delicious variation.

Makes 24

½ cup all-purpose flour

¼ cup cocoa powder

¼ teaspoon salt

¼ teaspoon baking powder

1 large egg

½ cup granulated sugar

1 teaspoon vanilla extract

¼ cup whole milk

¼ cup butter (½ stick), melted and cooled, plus more as needed

½ cup semisweet chocolate chips

1. In a medium bowl, combine the flour, cocoa powder, salt, and baking powder. Use a whisk to mix thoroughly. If the cocoa powder or baking powder is lumpy, sift the mixture.

2. In another medium bowl, whisk together the egg, sugar, vanilla extract, and milk. Drizzle in the cooled butter and whisk to combine. Stir the dry ingredients into the wet ingredients.

3. Brush the cups of the takoyaki pan with melted butter and heat the pan over medium-low heat. Using a small cookie scoop, drop batter into the first row of takoyaki cups, filling about ⅔ full. Immediately drop three chocolate chips into each cup, poking the chips to submerge them in the batter. Repeat to fill the remaining cups, one row at a time. Cook the rows for 4 to 5 minutes, until the undersides of the pops are dry and lightly browned. Use a pick to turn each bite over, and cook for 2 to 3 minutes more. Using two picks or chopsticks, remove from the pan and let cool slightly on a plate; serve warm.

SWEET CREAM AND BLUEBERRY DUMPLINGS

Who says dumplings need to be savory? Use the rest of your dumpling wrappers to make a fun dessert. Although blueberries are used in this recipe, you can also try it with raspberries or cut-up chunks of cherries or strawberries.

Makes 16

3 ounces cream cheese, softened

1 tablespoon powdered sugar

1 teaspoon whole milk

16 round gyoza wrappers

1/2 cup blueberries

2 tablespoons melted butter

1. In a small bowl, combine the cream cheese, powdered sugar, and milk. Mix it together with a spoon to make a smooth paste.

2. On a clean work surface, lay out a few gyoza wrappers. Place about 1/2 teaspoon of the cream cheese mixture in the center of each wrapper. Place a couple of blueberries on the cream cheese. Use your finger to wet the edges of the wrappers, then bunch up the edges into the middle to form a pouch. Press together to seal. Repeat with the remaining ingredients.

3. Brush the cups of the takoyaki pan with melted butter and heat the pan over medium-low heat. Place the dumplings into each cup of the takoyaki pan, pressing down lightly to make sure the dumplings make contact with the bottom of the cups. Cook for 2 to 3 minutes.

While the dumplings are cooking, brush the tops of the
dumplings lightly with butter. When the undersides of
the dumplings are crisp and brown, turn each over and
cook for 1 to 2 minutes more, until equally browned.
Using two picks or chopsticks, remove from the pan.
Let cool slightly before eating.

LINGONBERRY AEBLESKIVER

From a cultural and culinary standpoint, Japan and Sweden are very different. So I'm not sure how it came to be that both nations share such a similar cooking appliance. The takoyaki pan and the aebleskive pan are strikingly similar: both are a flat pan with a series of round indentations. They are also used in similar ways since batter is poured into the indentation, allowed to cook, and then gradually turned so that the batter flows to form a crispy sphere of goodness. But unlike savory takoyaki, aebleskiver (you make these treats plural with an *r* instead of an *s*) are sweet, more like a pancake, and in Swedish culture they are enjoyed as an afternoon snack with coffee or mulled wine. Though the pans look similar, there are indeed some minor differences: the indentations in the aebleskive pan are usually larger, making a bigger ball than takoyaki. The pans are usually also round, rather than square, and made from cast iron rather than aluminum like most takoyaki pans. Still, the pans are alike enough that I just had to include a riff on this strikingly similar snack.

Makes 32

1 cup all-purpose flour

1 tablespoon granulated sugar

1 teaspoon baking powder

1/2 teaspoon baking soda

1/4 teaspoon salt

1 egg, separated

1/2 cup whole milk

1/2 cup buttermilk

1/4 cup butter, melted and cooled slightly, plus more as needed

1/4 cup lingonberry jam

1/4 cup powdered sugar

1. In a medium bowl, combine the flour, granulated sugar, baking powder, baking soda, and salt. Whisk to combine. In a small bowl, whisk the egg yolk. Stir in the milk and buttermilk. Stir the milk mixture into the dry ingredients, stirring with a whisk or a fork just until combined. Drizzle the butter into the mixture and stir until combined.

2. With a whisk or a hand mixer, beat the egg white until fluffy. Fold into the batter.

3. Brush the cups of the takoyaki pan with melted butter and heat the pan over medium-low heat. Using a small cookie scoop, drop the batter into the cups. Spoon about ½ teaspoon lingonberry jam into each cup. Let cook for about 2 minutes, until the underside is crisp and lightly golden. Using a pick, carefully rotate each aebleskive halfway, letting the raw batter flow back into the pan, and then rotate all the way over. Cook for 1 to 2 minutes more until the underside is equally golden. Using two picks or chopsticks, remove from the pan. Sprinkle with powdered sugar and serve warm.

ABOUT THE AUTHOR

JESSICA HARLAN is the author of more than ten books, including *The Little Book of Takoyaki*. After receiving a degree in rhetoric from the University of Illinois, she revisited her love of food by getting a job as an assistant editor for a gourmet food trade magazine. Later, she moved to New York City and attended the Institute of Culinary Education to learn about professional cooking. She has written for About.com, *Clean Eating*, *Town & Country*, *Tasting Table*, *Consumers Digest*, *Time Out New York*, and others.

Jessicagoldbogen.com

AIMEE PONG is an artist and designer based in Brooklyn. Her work has been recognized by the Society of Illustrators, *3x3*, and Graphis. She is currently a designer at OrangeYouGlad and a contributing cartoonist for the *Lily* by the *Washington Post*.

MORE GREAT BOOKS
from Little, Brown Lab

CPSIA information can be obtained
at www.ICGtesting.com
Printed in the USA
LVHW040328190719
624577LV00002B/52/P

9 780316 494120